Soups
For Healthy Living

AYESHA DAVAR

Print information available on the last page

Rev. date: 06/28/2018

To order additional copies of this book, contact:
Xlibris
0800-056-3182
www.xlibrispublishing.co.uk
Orders@ Xlibrispublishing.co.uk

Contents

ABOUT THE AUTHOR

Ayesha Davar was born in 1942 and lived in India until 1966.

She moved to the United Kingdom with her family in 1967. In London, that time was the flower power era, and the Beatles (the famous pop group) were just beginning to climb the ladder.

Ayesha initially started by selling tie-dye and batik paintings at the famous Hyde Park Corner to introduce ethnic fashion in the West in 1967 with the Beatles Shop. She was encouraged by the director, Mr John Lyndon of the Beatles shop called Apple Boutique in Baker Street London to design clothes that the pop group were wearing–Indian kurtas, embroidered waistcoats, fully embroidered jackets, kaftans, etc.

Ayesha worked with her mother in India, who translated her designs and sent the shipments to her. She became famous for her unique designs under her own label, Ayesha Davar. Peter Simon, owner of Monsoon shops, visited her showroom/warehouse in Kilburn in 1971/1972 to buy many of her designs to sell in his shops. Many chains and stores bought her original designs, including Chelsea Girl (now renamed River Island), Oasis, Fenwicks, Miss Selfridge, etc. Ayesha was in the fashion business for over twenty-five years, running a successful wholesale, retail, exports, and mail order.

Ayesha had a passion for cooking. At the age of sixteen, after Ayesha finished school, her mother (who was a brilliant cook) sent her to a famous cookery chef and teacher Mrs Balbir Singh, in Rouse Avenue, New Delhi. Ayesha has retained all the recipes and her recipe book that she learnt from Mrs Singh in 1958.

Ayesha's mother visited the United Kingdom every year and taught her simple home-made recipes for everyday cooking, which are all saved in her own home recipe book as she also hopes to publish her mother's taught recipes. She is at her final stage of editing the simple easy dishes.

Ayesha has done catering for Middlesex Hospital NHS Trust, for nearly four years providing her own prepared dishes for the pharmacists every Wednesday on their meetings arranged by pharmaceutical companies such as Pfizer, Amgen, Merck Sharp & Dohme, etc. She was also invited to provide food for the doctors' meetings at St Mays Hospital Paddington, Whipps Cross Hospital, and many other hospitals.

She worked as a voluntary chef in Puttaparthi at the ashram of her guru, Sa Baba, in the foreign canteen. She prepared tofu, cabbage, and noodle soup; vegetarian paneer pancakes; chickpeas and split moong dhal; spinach soup; and various other dishes for around 200 devotees who visited the canteen.

Ayesha's little distribution set-up was called Diva Catering. It provided a few shops and private clients frozen dishes labelled and packed with a Dyno packing machine in 1997, at a time when plastic containers were not available.

Ayesha is very enterprising in many fields and has been instrumental in bringing many health carers and qualified nurses from abroad to the United Kingdom when there was a huge shortage of health carers and nurses in 2002 till 2006. She provided them with accommodation and food.

She then went on to open her own two private colleges as it was not possible to provide the health carers and nurses from outside Europe to find an adaptation course to work in hospitals and nursing homes and residential homes. She provided them with national vocational qualifications accredited by OCR (Oxford and Cambridge).

For some time, Ayesha had been trying to lose weight to control her cholesterol and high blood pressure. Her daughter Zareena Cuddis, a medical doctor, prepared a healthy pea-and-mint soup, and the idea to have such a quick and hassle-free simple recipe gave her the idea to create and prepare soups in a soup maker.

It has helped her lose weight and feel healthy. Her sugar levels have reduced several units, and that encouraged her to write the book on soups.

Soups made from fresh vegetables are healthy. It increases the energy level. She feels less bloated, and her skin has improved. In her own words: "I could now never do without a soup daily. A soup maker is indispensable."

This book contains thirty-one recipes—one for each day of the month. All the recipes have been personally tested, tried, taught, and relished time and again.

Some of the soups she has introduced a little more spice, turmeric, ground coriander, roasted cumin powder, and even a fresh green chilli. You can always increase the spice quota if you enjoy the spices. Once you use the soup maker, you will feel the benefits of the soups. There is not a day in the year that you would want to do without it.

Souping is the healthy way of dieting and provides nourishment while helping you to lose weight. It's a great choice if you want to lose weight healthily.

Hope you enjoy all the recipes in this book and reap the benefits of healthy ingredients. Have a healthy living!

CREDITS

First, I would like to acknowledge and give credit to my Grandson Krish Puri, who designed the cover and prepared the website AyeshaDavar.com. At the very early age of eleven years, he started to make short films. Now that he's aged fourteen years, there is not an occasion where he has not prepared a film (surprising the family)—he does films for family birthdays, cruises, Christmas, New Year parties, etc. He runs a small studio called Puri Studios and has designed his own website. You can view his short films on YouTube. Feel free to contact him at puristudios12@gmail.com.

I thank my granddaughter Tanya Puri, who tries and tests all the spices and gives me a feedback.

I also would like to thank all my family, who have been a great support in testing the soups and appreciating the combinations and additions of great-flavoured Indian spices!

Ayesha Davar

INTRODUCTION

Soup is a quick, hot meal that offers plenty of health benefits. Soup is incredibly easy to prepare, especially in a soup maker. Soups are healthy, economical, and low in calories. You can use up leftovers you have in the kitchen and create variations of favourite recipes since soup lends itself to experimentations. Soups can be easily frozen.

Advantages of soups are many just to name a few.

- Less stress

- Energy all day

- Less bloating

- Glowing skin

- A flatter tummy

- Natural weight loss

The recipes in this book are mostly written for use with a soup maker but can be prepared in the traditional method of boiling on the cooker and then blended in a mixer.

Making them in a soup maker takes away the hard work. You don't have to be a great chef to make incredible soups using a soup maker. A great choice! The jug-style soup maker is unquestionably one of the best- and easiest-performing device on the market.

It is really quick—not much preparation and no mess. Put all the ingredients in with stock, press a button, and come back in thirty minutes to a piping-hot delicious soup.

Soup can be a perfect meal, a starter, or a snack all year round. Soups can be enjoyed whatever time of the year. Soups can help in losing weight and maintaining your figure. Using all fresh ingredients makes it a winner for a healthy and balanced diet.

All the recipes in my book are low-calorie. These recipes are good for people suffering from diabetes, high blood pressure, and high cholesterol.

If you struggle to eat your five-a-day, then a bowl of soup usually provides at least two portions.

SOUP BASE

Onion, leek, potato, and celery are good ingredients for a base.

STOCK

Good-quality stock cubes like Oxo or Maggie will make your soup tastier. Choose stock cubes that are not high in sodium.

Home-Made Vegetable Stock

INGREDIENTS

2 tbsp olive oil

4 garlic cloves

1 leek, chopped

1 onion, chopped

2 bay leaves

2 carrots, chopped

2 sticks celery

4 tomatoes, diced

8 mushrooms

2 tbsp parsley leaves, chopped

10 cups water

Add the olive oil, add chopped onions, leek, carrots, garlic cloves, and sweat for 3–4 minutes.

Add all the other ingredients, cover and bring to boil, leave to gently simmer for 15 minutes.

Allow to cool for a little while.

Pour the contents through a sieve and store in the fridge use for 3–4 days or freeze in ice cube trays.

Home-Made Chicken Stock

INGREDIENTS

2 tbsp olive oil

2 carrots, chopped

1 leek, chopped

leftover bones from chicken carcass

2 onions, chopped

2 garlic cloves, crushed

2 stalks celery, chopped

8 black peppercorns

2 bay leaves

2 tbsp parsley leaves, chopped

12 cups water

Sauté the onions, leek, and garlic in olive oil, then add all the other ingredients in a large saucepan. Break the chicken carcass into pieces and add to the pan. Cover and bring to a boil. Cook for a minimum of 1 hour. Simmer for 1 hour. Pour contents in a sieve, let it cool, and freeze in ice cube trays.

SEASONING

Garlic, ginger, and coriander work well as seasoning. If you like your soups with a little more flavour, you can add parsley, oregano, thyme, sage, etc.

To give it an Asian flavour, you could add ground roasted cumin, turmeric, ground coriander, or garam masala (all spice). A green chilli chopped can add even more zest.

GARNISH

Freshly chopped herbs such as coriander leaves, basil leaves, chives, and tarragon leaves give a finishing touch to your soups. Adding croutons, crème fraiche, Greek yogurt, or freshly grated Parmesan cheese. All add to the taste.

HOME-MADE CROUTONS

1. Preheat oven to 250°F degrees

2. Remove crusts from bread slices. Brush bread on both sides with melted butter. Cut bread slices into small cubes.

3. Bake at 250°F for 5 minutes, remove tray carefully toss croutons. Bake for another 5 minutes or until browned. Let it cool then store croutons in a tight-lid container.

GARLIC CROUTONS

2 cloves garlic, crushed

3 slices of white bread

3 tbsp olive oil

Remove crusts from bread slice. Cut the bread into small cubes.

Mix the above ingredients. Add the cubes and mix well.

Heat the oven to 180 and bake the cubes in a baking tray. When the cubes are golden brown, remove and drain on kitchen paper towel.

Sprinkle salt and pepper and red chilli powder if desired.

STORE CUPBOARD ESSENTIALS

1   BAY LEAF
2   BULGUR WHEAT
3   CINNAMON STICKS
4   CHICKPEAS
5   SWEET CORN TINS
6   SOYA SAUCE
7   OLIVES (BLACK, GREEN)
8   LEMON JUICE
9   OLIVE OIL
10 GARAM MASALA (ALL SPICE)
11 *DHANIYA* (GROUND CORIANDER)
12 CUMIN POWDER
13 PEARL BARLEY
14 RED LENTIL
15 SPLIT GREEN DHAL
16 BLACK PEPPER
17 RED CHILLI POWDER
18 OREGANO
19 THYME
20 NUTMEG POWDER
21 DRIED CHIVES

22 MIXED HERBS
23 GROUND TUMERIC
24 SESAME OIL
25 SUNFLOWER OIL
26 CHICKEN STOCK CUBES
27 VEGETABLE STOCK CUBES
28 BEEF STOCK CUBES
29 ASAFOETIDA
30 WALNUT
31 ALMOND
32 PINE NUTS
33 VINEGAR

LIQUID MEASURES

¼ PINT	145 millilitre
½ PINT	285 millilitre
1 ¾ PINT	1000 millilitre

MEASUREMENTS AND WEIGHTS

5 grams	1 teaspoon
15 grams	1 tablespoon
100 grams	½ cup
225 grams	1 cup

OVEN TEMPERATURE

OVEN	F	C	GAS MARKS
SLOW	300	120	1, 2
MODERATE	375	160	3, 4
HOT	450	200	5, 6
VERY HOT	500	240	8, 9

SOUP MAKER

AUBERGINE AND MUSHROOM SOUP

INGREDIENTS

1 large aubergine

4 garlic cloves

2 tbsp olive oil

1 cup freshly chopped mushroom

2 medium-sized onions (preferably purple)

2 tsp ground coriander

2 tsp lemon juice

1 cup plain low fat yogurt

2 tsp roasted ground cumin

1 vegetable stock cube

600 ml water

½ green chilli, chopped

1 tbsp garam masala

salt and pepper to taste

METHOD

Trim the stalks from the aubergine.

Apply oil to the aubergine and cook in microwave till the skin can be peeled off.

Cut the aubergine into cubes after removing the skin.

If you have the sauté function on the soup maker, then add the olive oil and sauté the garlic and finely chopped onions.

Add the cubed aubergines, and all the other ingredients except the lemon juice.

Press the Creamed setting. Swirl in the lemon juice.

GARNISH

Ladle the soup into bowls and sprinkle black pepper. You may also sprinkle chopped coriander leaves.

PROPERTIES

Aubergine is beneficial for weight loss. Also it is good for healthy digestion and normalizes iron level. Eggplant, as it commonly called, is low in calories.

NOURISHING AVOCADO CREAMY SOUP

INGREDIENTS

2 avocado, peeled and chopped

1 leek, peeled and chopped

2 cups low-fat yogurt

150 ml water

salt and pepper

1 wedge Laughing Cow Cheese

1 chicken or vegetable stock cube

2 tbsp coriander leaves, chopped

2 tbsp lemon juice

METHOD

Add the above ingredients except the coriander and lemon juice.

Choose the Creamed setting on the soup maker.

The soup will be ready in about 25 minutes.

Open the lid and add the chopped coriander leaves and the lemon juice.

GARNISH

Sprinkle each bowl with more coriander chopped leaves and fresh grated black pepper.

PROPERTIES

Avocado is very filling and full of nutritional properties that help people lose weight. Avocados do not contain any cholesterol or sodium and are low in saturated fat.

BOK CHOY SPICY GREEN SOUP

INGREDIENTS

250 g bok choy, sliced

75 g broccoli, chopped

½ green chilli

3 garlic cloves, crushed

1 small potato

2 tbsp lemon juice

2 tsp sugar

2 tsp grated ginger

500 ml vegetable stock

750 g frozen peas

salt and pepper to taste

METHOD

Add all the above ingredients to the soup maker except the lemon juice.

Choose the stock cube with little or no sodium.

Choose the Creamed setting on the soup maker, and in 20–25 minutes, the soup should be ready.

Mix in the lemon juice.

Garnish

Sprinkle some chopped coriander leaves and ground black pepper.

PROPERTIES

Nutritionally, bok choy is loaded with cancer-fighting properties. It is very low in calories but is a rich source of vitamin A and vitamin C.

BROCCOLI AND BLUE LAUGHING COW CHEESE SOUP

INGREDIENTS

350 broccoli into florets

1 leek, chopped

1 small potato

1 onion, chopped

1 tbsp olive oil

salt and pepper to taste

2 tsp butter

700 ml water

4 tbsp single low-fat cream

2 tbsp mascarpone cheese

2 wedges blue Laughing Cow Cheese

METHOD

Place the butter and olive oil in the soup maker.

Add the broccoli, potato, leek, onion, and water in the jug.

Turn on the soup maker. When finished, open, add the single cream, and stir in the cheese until the cheese is melted—choose the Blend setting.

For ease, you could stir in the cheese and single cream with all the ingredients using hot water.

GARNISH

Add to each bowl a teaspoon of mascarpone cheese.

PROPERTIES

Broccoli is low in calories and high in fibre, vitamins, and minerals. It contains significant amounts of fibre to facilitate better digestion. Increasing broccoli in your diet may help to slow down and prevent osteoarthritis. It prevents heart disease and contains lutein, which may help prevent thickening of the arteries

CARROT AND CORIANDER SOUP

INGREDIENTS

8–9 carrots chopped

1 onion, chopped

1 potato, chopped

1 tsp butter

1 leek, chopped

1 chicken or vegetable stock cube

1 tsp ground coriander

400 ml water

1 tsp grated ginger

1 green chilli, chopped

2 tbsp fresh coriander, chopped

1 tsp salt and ½ tsp pepper

½ tsp garam masala

2 tbsp fresh lemon juice

METHOD

Add all the above ingredients to the soup maker.

Stir with a wooden spoon

Always make sure the ingredients do not exceed the maximum level as shown inside the jug.

Choose the Cream setting and press the start button

After 20–25 minutes there will be a bleep sound, and the soup is ready.

GARNISH

Garnish with more coriander and black pepper. Optional you could add 1 tsp single cream to each bowl.

PROPERTIES

Carrots are rich in beta-carotene and fibre content. Furthermore, carrots are rich in vitamin A, vitamin C, vitamin K, vitamin B_8, potassium, iron, copper, and manganese. It also helps in improving the immune system. The abundance of vitamin A in carrot juice can help improve your sight, and daily intake can prevent the onset of heart disease and stroke.

CAULIFLOWER AND STILTON BLUE CHEESE SOUP

INGREDIENTS

400 g cauliflower
(cut into florets)
1 medium-sized onion, chopped
1 medium-sized potato, chopped
1 leek, chopped
1 bay leaf
1 tsp garam masala (all spice)
2 tbsp fresh coriander, chopped

50 g stilton cheese or mature cheddar
1 tbsp olive oil or vegetable oil
1 vegetable stock cube, dissolved in 400 ml water
2 cloves garlic, crushed
1 green chilli, chopped
1 cup skimmed milk
salt and pepper to taste

METHOD

Add all the above ingredients to your soup maker except the fresh coriander leaves.
Choose the Creamed setting.
When the soup is ready, it will bleep about 20–25 minutes.
Before the programme finishes, you will hear the blending sound, and after that, a bleep.
It will then go to Warm and keep the soup hot for 40 minutes.

GARNISH

Ladle the soup into bowls and sprinkle with chopped coriander leaves.

PROPERTIES

Cauliflower is low in calories. It is loaded with vitamin C, potassium, fibre, and folic acid. Cauliflower is low in saturated fat and cholesterol and is a good source of protein.

CREAM OF COURGETTE SOUP

INGREDIENTS

3 medium-sized courgettes, chopped
(also called zucchini)

1 medium-sized onion

1 small potato

1 leek, chopped

1 green chilli, chopped

2 vegetable stock cube

400 ml water

2 tbsp coriander leaves, chopped

salt and pepper to taste

2 triangles blue Laughing Cow Cheese
or 2 tbsp crème fraiche

This soup is very easy to make and perfect and delicious light for lunch. You will want to make it time and time again.

METHOD

Add the onion, cream cheese, potato, courgette, half the coriander leaves, salt, pepper and water in the appliance.

Choose the Creamed setting.

GARNISH

Sprinkle black pepper and coriander leaves.

PROPERTIES OF COURGETTES

Courgettes or zucchini is a well-known weight-loss food. They contain soluble fibre, which slows down digestion and so stabilises blood sugar and insulin levels. Soluble fibre also helps prevent constipation and relieves irritable bowel syndrome. Courgettes contain vitamin K, vitamin C, and dietary fibre.

RED CABBAGE, YOGURT, AND ROASTED CUMIN SOUP

INGREDIENTS

1½ lb or 1 small head red cabbage

1 onion, diced

1 tbsp butter

½ tsp garam masala (all spice)

¼ tsp roasted cumin seeds

1 small potato

2 tbsp fresh lemon juice

1 tbsp olive oil

1 tsp ground turmeric

1 vegetable stock cube

5 cups water

1 tbsp honey

1 Granny Smith apple

(peeled and cored)

1 cup low-fat plain yoghurt

1 tsp ground coriander powder

salt and pepper to taste

METHOD

Add the olive oil and butter. Add the onion, chopped cabbage and all other ingredients except the lemon juice and yoghurt.

Choose the Creamed setting. When the soup is ready, stir in the yogurt.

GARNISH

Add 1 tsp of lemon juice to each bowl and sprinkle garam masala on top.

PROPERTES

Red cabbage is very good for the skin. The health benefit of red cabbage includes prevention of premature aging. Cabbage has no cholesterol or saturated fat and is very low in calories.

CORIANDER, CABBAGE, AND LEMON SOUP

INGREDIENTS

1 bunch coriander, chopped (include half the stalks)

1 onion, chopped

2 cups cabbage, chopped

3 cloves garlic, crushed

½ tsp red chilli powder

1 tbsp gram flour

1 tsp ground coriander

1 tsp ground turmeric

1 vegetable stock cube

1 tsp roasted ground cumin

400 ml water

1 cup plain yoghurt

4 tbsp lemon juice

salt and pepper to taste

METHOD

Add all the above ingredients to the soup maker.

Choose the Creamed setting. After 25 minutes, a lovely flavoured soup will be ready.

GARNISH

To serve, ladle the soup into bowls, stir a teaspoon of lemon juice in each bowl, and top each bowl with fresh chopped coriander leaves.

PROPERTIES

Coriander (also known as cilantro) gives multiple health benefits. All over the world, it is known for its medicinal properties. Coriander leaves are rich in vitamin C, vitamin K, and protein. It is considered a very good cleanse for the kidneys.

CREAMY CELERIAC SOUP
WITH ROASTED CUMIN

INGREDIENTS

1 medium-sized celeriac, chopped

1 celery stick, sliced

1 medium-sized onion, chopped

1 apple, peeled and cored

Salt and pepper to taste

1 tsp ground coriander

1 leek, chopped

500 ml water

1 vegetable stock cube

1 tsp roasted ground cumin

2 tbsp mascarpone cheese

1 tsp roasted ground cumin

4 tbsp low-fat yoghurt

1 tbsp fresh coriander, chopped

METHOD

Add the above ingredients to the soup maker, except the mascarpone cheese and roasted cumin seeds.

Choose the Creamed setting.

When it has finished cooking, open the lid. Add the mascarpone cheese.

Choose the Blend setting.

Serve the soups in bowls.

GARNISH

Sprinkle the roasted cumin powder and chopped coriander on top.

PROPERTIES

Celeriac is low in calories. Celeriac is a very good source of vitamin K.

HOT CUCUMBER AND PEARL BARLEY SOUP

INGREDIENTS

1 medium-sized cucumber

1 leek, chopped

2 garlic cloves, crushed

½ in. ginger crushed

1 tsp sesame oil

½ green chilli, chopped

1 tbsp soya sauce

1 tsp garam masala (all spice)

500 ml chicken or vegetable stock

½ cup barley, washed and soaked for ½ hour

½ tsp salt

½ tsp freshly ground black pepper

2 tbsp crème fraiche

METHOD

Add all the above ingredients to the soup maker except the garam masala and crème fraiche.

Choose the Creamed setting. When finished, open the lid and add garam masala and the crème fraiche. Choose the Blend setting.

GARNISH

Ladle the soup in the bowls and swirl a dash of crème fraiche.

PROPERTIES

Cucumber is a natural diuretic and helps reduce water retention. This soup is perfect for when you feel bloated. Barley lowers the cholesterol level and therefore reduces the risk of coronary heart disease.

ROASTED GARLIC WITH PARMESAN CHEESE

INGREDIENTS

25 roasted garlic cloves

2 tbsp olive oil

½ tsp freshly ground black pepper

1 chicken stock cube

600 ml water

½ cup grated parmesan cheese

½ cup flour

½ cup low-fat single cream

1 onion, chopped

15 garlic cloves, raw, chopped

3 tbsp lemon juice

2 tbsp butter

METHOD

Preheat oven to 350°F. Place 25 garlic cloves in a baking dish and drizzle olive oil.

Sprinkle with ½ tsp salt and black pepper.

Cover glass baking dish with kitchen foil and bake for 25 minutes.

Add all the above ingredients to the soup maker, including the roasted garlic cloves and the chopped garlic cloves. Add plain flour mixed in cold water.

Do not add the parmesan cheese and lemon juice.

The soup will be ready in about 25 minutes.

Add the lemon juice and choose the Blend setting.

GARNISH

Sprinkle the grated parmesan cheese and freshly ground black pepper.

PROPERTIES

Garlic contains a compound called allicin. It has many medicinal properties. Garlic is widely used for several conditions linked to the blood system and heart, including high cholesterol and coronary heart disease. It is the perfect natural antibiotic, which helps build up your immune system and helps fight of colds and flu. Garlic contains vitamin C, vitamin B_6, manganese, and calcium.

LEEK AND BLUE LAUGHING COW CHEESE SOUP

INGREDIENTS

3 leeks, peeled and chopped

1 medium potato, chopped

1 onion, chopped

1 tbsp olive oil

1 tbsp cornflour mixed in water

salt and pepper to taste

2 cups vegetable stock

2 wedges blue Laughing Cow Cheese or
60 g mature cheddar cheese

1 tbsp Dijon mustard

2 garlic cloves, crushed

1 tbsp oregano

METHOD

Add all the ingredients in the soup maker.

Mix the cornflour with a bit of water.

Stir with a wooden spoon. Do not go past the maximum line in your soup maker.

Choose the Creamed setting.

The soup will be ready in about 25 minutes, when the bleep will sound.

GARNISH

Sprinkle with ground walnut powder and a pinch of black pepper.

PROPERTIES

Leeks belong to the family of garlic and onions. Leeks are excellent source of vitamin K, omega-3, and fatty acids, and is a source of vitamin C, vitamin A, and Vitamin E. Fresh leeks should be stored unwashed and untrimmed in the refrigerator where they will keep fresh for up to two weeks.

MOONG GREENS, SPLIT DHAL, AND SPINACH SOUP

INGREDIENTS

2 bunches roughly chopped spinach (palak)

1 green chilli

1 tsp ground turmeric

½ cup green split lentil (dhal)

1 tsp grated ginger

500 ml water

1 vegetable stock cube

salt to taste

2 tbsp ghee

2 cloves garlic, chopped

1 tiny pinch asafoetida

1 medium-sized onion, chopped

1 tsp ground coriander

¼ tsp red chilli powder

½ red chili flakes

1 tbsp fresh coriander, chopped

METHOD

Soak moong dhal overnight or two hours before preparing the soup.

Add all the ingredients on the left-hand side in the soup maker.

When the soup is ready, in a frying pan, add ghee. Once it's hot, add the garlic cloves. Once they are brown, add the asafoetida. Add the onions. When the onions are half-brown, add the ground coriander, chilli flakes, and red chilli powder.

Stir this mixture in the ready soup.

GARNISH

Sprinkle with fresh chopped coriander leaves.

PROPERTIES

Green moong dhal is a superfood for weight loss. A bowl of moong dhal is less than 110 calories. It is rich source of protein. Spinach (palak) is rich in iron, and its juice is good for the skin and hair, and is also good for weight loss.

CREAM OF MUSHROOM AND HERB SOUP

INGREDIENTS

500 g white button or common mushrooms

½ leek, chopped

2 garlic cloves, crushed

1 tbsp olive oil

3 cups vegetable stock

salt and pepper to taste

½ green chilli, chopped

1 cup low-fat milk

1 tbsp plain flour

1 celery stick, chopped

¼ tsp dried thyme

1/2 low-fat single cream

pinch of ground nutmeg

2 tbsp fresh coriander leaves, chopped

2 wedges light Laughing Cow Cheese

Low-fat milk and plain flour paste provide the creaminess to the soup. The Laughing Cow Cheese is very low in fat. Weight Watchers recommends Laughing Cow Cheese.

METHOD

Add all the above ingredients to the soup maker except the single cream.

Choose the Creamed setting. When it has finished, pour it in the bowls, and swirl 1 tsp single cream in each bowl.

Cheese.

GARNISH

Serve with chopped coriander leaves sprinkled on top and add home-made croutons.

PROPERTIES

Mushrooms are low in calories and cholesterol-free. Eating mushrooms helps improve nutrition. Mushrooms play an important role in helping the immune system fight diseases such as cancer. They are becoming more popular for their disease-fighting and health-protecting properties.

CREAMY PARSNIP AND ROASTED CUMIN SOUP

INGREDIENTS

3 parsnips, chopped

2 tbsp olive oil

2 tsp roasted ground cumin

2 onions, chopped

4 garlic cloves, chopped

1 tsp ground coriander

½ tsp turmeric

salt and pepper to taste

3 cups vegetable stock

1 small potato

½ green chilli, chopped

2 tbsp fresh coriander, chopped

¼ cup low-fat single cream

1 tsp garam masala

METHOD

Add the olive oil and onions in your soup maker. Add all the ingredients, except the single cream and only 1 tbsp chopped fresh coriander.

Choose the Creamed setting. When the function is finished, add the single cream and choose the Blend setting.

GARNISH

Serve in bowls and sprinkle the chopped coriander leaves. Sprinkle ground roasted cumin seed powder.

Roasted ground cumin

Take 2 teaspoons of whole cumin and put it in a frying pan on the hob. When they start to pop

Just cool them and add it to the grinder.

PROPERTIES

Celeriac has diuretic properties. The herb can help prevent excess water retention in the body. It also has anticancer properties. Celery root has excellent calming, anti-allergic, and other therapeutic properties.

Garnish

Stir a swirl of crème fraiche and a good grinding of black pepper.

PROPERTIES

Sweet potatoes is rich source of anti-oxidants, vitamins (richest source of vitamin A), minerals, and dietary fibre. Sweet potatoes are packed with calcium, potassium, and vitamin A and C.

SWEDE AND CARROT SOUP

INGREDIENTS

1 large swede, peeled and chopped

4 medium-sized carrots, chopped

1 medium onion, chopped

2 tbsp olive oil

salt and pepper to taste

3 garlic cloves, crushed

1 vegetable stock cube

2 tbsp crème fraiche

500 ml water

METHOD

Add all the above ingredients to the soup maker except the crème fraiche.

Choose the Creamed setting. Press the button and then press Start.

The soup will be ready in 25 minutes.

When the soup is ready, the soup maker will bleep and then go on to the Keep Warm setting.

It will remain hot for 40 minutes.

GARNISH

Ladle the soup into bowls and swirl in some crème fraiche.

PROPERTIES

Swede is a root vegetable and provides many health benefits as it is a good source of vitamins and nutrients. Swede is rich in vitamin A and vitamin C. This sweet-flavoured vegetable provides a rich source of fibre.

SPICY SWEET POTATO AND COCONUT MILK

INGREDIENTS

2 large sweet potatoes, peeled and cubed

2 medium-sized carrots, peeled and chopped

2 onions, chopped

1 leek, chopped

4 garlic cloves, crushed

1 tbsp ginger, grated

2 tbsp fresh coriander leaves, chopped

2 tbsp fresh lemon juice

1 cup coconut milk

1 vegetable stock cube

3 cups water

2 tsp sesame oil

1 tbsp sunflower oil

1 tsp ground coriander

1 tbsp garam masala (all spice)

½ tsp red chilli powder

salt and pepper to taste

METHOD

Heat the oven to 200°C. Add to a baking bowl sweet potatoes and carrots.

Drizzle the olive oil and bake for 25 minutes.

Add the sesame oil to a pan, add the onions and leek, and fry till lightly brown.

Add the baked vegetables to the soup maker and all the above ingredients except the coconut milk and fresh coriander.

Choose the Creamed setting, and the soup will be ready in 25 minutes.

Stir through the coconut milk.

GARNISH

To serve, ladle the soup into bowls and top each bowl with a spoonful of fresh coriander leaves.

PROPERTIES

Sweet potato is a rich source of vitamin A and vitamin C, calcium, potassium, and dietary fibre.

CREAMY PARVAR (POINTED GOURD) SOUP

CREAM OF TOMATO AND BASIL SOUP

INGREDIENTS

6–7 vine tomatoes

1 garlic clove

1 level tbsp cornflour

500 ml vegetable stock

1 small onion

1 tsp sugar

1 tbsp of butter

2 tbsp mascarpone cheese

10 torn basil leaves

salt and pepper to taste

ground pine nuts for garnishing

METHOD

Tomatoes: With a knife, take out the green eyes of the tomatoes, and place in a bowl. Pour boiling water over the tomatoes, and after 30 seconds, run cold water. Peel away the skins and chop into quarters.

Mix the cornflour with a little water. Put the tomatoes, onion, garlic, butter, blended cornflour, mascarpone cheese, basil leaves, and vegetable stock in the soup maker.

Salt lightly, as the stock will be a bit salty, and season with ground black pepper.

Choose the Creamed soup setting. After about 25 minutes, the soup will be ready.

GARNISH

Sprinkle ground pine nuts, add a basil leaf in the centre, and sprinkle black pepper. You could add a few croutons.

Croutons: Take a slice of bread and cut small squares. Put in an oven at 200°C for about 10 minutes. Usually I prepare 10 slices of plain white bread and store them in an airtight container, and they are always ready to add to various soups.

PROPERTIES

Tomatoes are very good for the skin. They contain lycopene, which is also used for facial cleansers. Tomatoes contain vitamin C, vitamin K, manganese, dietary fibre, and vitamin A.

ROASTED FENNEL AND CARROT SOUP

INGREDIENTS

4 carrots, peeled and chopped

2 bulbs of fennel, trimmed and sliced

1 large onion, chopped

6 cloves garlic in their skin/jackets

1 tsp dried thyme

3 tbsp olive oil

2 bay leaves

600 ml water

2 vegetable stock cube

3 tbsp low-fat single cream

2 tbsp crème fraiche

salt and pepper to taste

½ green chilli chopped

METHOD

Preheat oven to 200°C

Toss the chopped carrots, fennel, dried thyme, bay leaves, and onion in a roasting dish.

Drizzle olive oil and season with salt and pepper.

Roast for 25 minutes. Then add the garlic cloves in their skin. Return them to oven for another 15 minutes or until the vegetables are soft.

Add the above ingredients (remove the skin of the garlic cloves) except the crème fraiche to the soup maker.

Press the Creamed setting, and the soup will be ready in about 25 minutes.

Add boiling water if the soup is too thick to the consistency required.

GARNISH

Pour the soup in bowls and serve with a swirl of crème fraiche.

PROPERTIES

The health benefits of fennel include relief from anaemia, indigestion, and constipation. It contains significant amounts of fibre, which helps lower cholesterol, thereby decreasing the risk of heart disease.

CHILLED SOUPS

If it is hot and you are in need of something light, tasty, and refreshing then chilled soup is the perfect answer—so cool, so healthy, and so invigorating with their aromatic and peppery flavours.

REFRESHING CHILLED ASPARAGUS SOUP

INGREDIENTS

8–10 fresh asparagus spears

1 leek, chopped

2 tbsp olive oil

2 tbsp cornflour mixed in water

2 garlic cloves, crushed

½ cup plain yogurt

5 cup water

1 vegetable stock cube

2 tbsp parsley, chopped (optional)

salt and pepper to taste

METHOD

Cut the top and trim the ends of the stalks, removing all brown or woody parts.

Add all the above ingredients to the soup maker except the parsley and yogurt.

Choose the Creamed setting.

When the soup is ready, stir in half the yogurt and half of the parsley.

When it is room temperature, cover the bowls and place in the refrigerator to chill thoroughly.

GARNISH

To serve, fill the individual bowls with the soup and place a spoonful of yogurt in the centre of each bowl. Sprinkle with the reserved parsley.

PROPERTIES

Asparagus is an excellent source of vitamin K, vitamin C, and vitamin E. It is a very good source of dietary fibre, manganese, zinc, iron, and vitamin B_6.

CHILLED AVOCADO SOUP

INGREDIENTS

2 medium ripe avocados, seeded and chopped

1/2 cup cucumber, chopped

½ cup spring onions, coarsely chopped

1 tsp salt

½ tsp black pepper

1 celery stick, chopped

3 cups water

1 vegetable stock cube

1 cup plain low-fat yogurt

2 tbsp dry sherry (optional)

METHOD

Add all the above ingredients except the yogurt and half the spring onions.

Choose the Creamed or Smooth setting.

When the soup is ready, stir in half the plain yogurt.

When it cools down to room temperature, cover the bowl and place in the refrigerator to chill thoroughly.

GARNISH

Ladle the soup into bowls. Place a spoonful of yogurt in the centre and swirl with a spoon.

Sprinkle with the remaining chopped spring onions.

CHILLED CUCUMBER AND PEA SOUP

INGREDIENTS

3 cups frozen peas

1 onion, chopped

1 large cucumber or 3 small cucumbers, chopped

400 ml water

1 tbsp soy sauce

20 fresh mint leaves

2 tbsp lemon juice

1 tsp sugar

1 tsp coarse-grain mustard

salt and pepper to taste

METHOD

Add the above ingredients in the soup maker except sugar, mint leaves, and lemon juice.

Choose the Creamed soup setting.

Open the soup maker and add the sugar, mint leaves, and the lemon juice.

Choose the Blend setting.

When the soup is room temperature, place in the fridge for 4 hours until the soup is cooled.

Serve chilled.

REFRESHING TOMATO SOUP

INGREDIENT

7–8 ripe tomatoes

1 tbsp olive oil

1 medium-sized onion, chopped

2 tbsp plain yogurt

1 vegetable stock cube

¼ tsp ground thyme

2 garlic cloves, crushed

1 bay leaf

¼ tsp oregano

500 ml water

2 tbsp crème fraiche

1 medium carrot, chopped

METHOD

Pour boiling water on the tomatoes and peel the skin.

Add the olive oil, onion, carrot, and all other ingredients except the crème fraiche.

Press the Smooth setting when the soup is ready, discard the bay leaf.

Leave to cool, then chill in the refrigerator.

GARNISH

Ladle the soup in the bowls and garnish with crème fraiche.

SOUPS WITH CHUNKY PIECES

ALL THE SOUPS IN THIS BOOK ARE LOW-CALORIE!

CHICKPEA, GARLIC, AND SPINACH SOUP

INGREDIENTS

1 can 400 g chickpeas

1 bunch spinach chopped

1 tbsp olive oil

3 garlic cloves crushed

1 onion chopped

2 tsp ginger grated

salt and pepper to taste

2 tbsp fresh coriander chopped

1 tsp cumin powder

1 tsp ground coriander

1 tsp garam masala

1 vegetable stock cube

500 ml water

1 green chilli chopped

2 tbsp lemon juice

METHOD

Add the olive oil to the soup maker.

If you have the Sauté function in the soup maker, add chopped onions, ginger, and garlic, and add the ground spices.

Sauté for 4–5 minutes.

The other alternative is to fry the above ingredients in a frying pan.

Add all the above ingredients to the soup maker. Choose the Chunky setting.

After 20–25 minutes, the soup will be ready.

GARNISH

Ladle the soup into soup bowls. Sprinkle with fresh chopped coriander.

Add lemon juice to each bowl.

CHINESE CHICKEN AND SWEET CORN SOUP

INGREDIENTS

1 can sweet corn

1 garlic clove, crushed

150 g chicken, shredded

2 spring onions

1 chicken stock cube

½ red chilli, seeded and chopped

900 ml water

salt and pepper to taste

1 purple onion, chopped

1 tsp grated ginger

2 tsp soya sauce

½ cup mushrooms, thinly sliced

2 tsp sesame oil

1 tbsp cornflour mixed in water

2 tbsp coriander, chopped

METHOD

Place the sweet corn kernels, red onion, garlic, cooked chicken, mushrooms, ginger, and spring onions into the soup maker.

Choose the Chunky setting.

The soup will be ready in about 25 minutes.

GARNISH

Swirl in a egg yolk in the figure of 8.

Sprinkle with 1 tsp spring onions. Top with a teaspoon of chopped fresh coriander leaves.

PRAWN, GINGER, AND COCONUT SOUP

INGREDIENTS

2 large garlic cloves

½ inch ginger, peeled and crushed

18 king-sized prawns, shelled

1 white onion, chopped

2 tbsp sesame oil

300 ml coconut milk

1 celery stick, sliced

½ green chilli

1 carrot, diced to tiny pieces

400 ml water

2 tbsp fresh coriander, chopped

salt and pepper to taste

METHOD

Add the sesame oil and the chopped onion, crushed ginger, small pieces of carrot, chilli powder, garlic cloves, and the prawns in small pieces. Keep 4 whole prawns to garnish.

Add the coconut milk and water.

Season with salt and pepper.

Choose the Soup with Pieces setting.

After 25 minutes, the soup is ready.

GARNISH

Ladle the soup into bowls and top each bowl with a single whole prawn. Sprinkle with chopped coriander leaves.

PROPERTIES

Prawns provide high quality protein, vitamins, and minerals. They are low in calories and are made of extremely healthy cholesterol.

CHICKEN AND GREEK YOGURT SOUP

INGREDIENTS

150 g chicken, boiled and chopped in tiny pieces

100 g frozen peas

1 carrot, chopped to tiny pieces

½ tsp mixed herbs

2 cloves garlic, crushed

1 tbsp olive oil

1 litre chicken stock

2 tbsp Greek yogurt, beaten

1/2 green chilli, chopped

½ tsp garam masala (all spice)

2 tbsp lemon juice

salt and pepper to taste

METHOD

Boil the chicken and chop to tiny pieces.

Pour boiling water on the frozen peas by placing in the colander.

Chop the carrot to tiny pieces, the size of chickpeas.

Add all the above ingredients, olive oil, chopped onions, crushed garlic, frozen peas, carrot, mixed herbs, chicken stock, green chilli, garam masala, and salt and pepper to taste.

Choose the Soup with Pieces setting.

When the soup is ready, open the lid, add the lemon juice, and add the beaten Greek yogurt.

Serve hot in soup bowls. It is optional to garnish with freshly chopped coriander leaves.

GLOSSARY

ENGLISH	HINDI
DRIED MANGO POWDER	AMCHOOR
CORIANDER LEAVES	DHANIYA
BOTTLE GOURD	LAUKI, DUDHI, GHIA
ALL SPICE	GARAM MASALA
CUMIN	ZEERA
SPLIT GREEN DHAL	MUNG DHAL
SPINACH	PALAK
MINT LEAVES	PUDINA
SWEET POTATO	SAKARKANDI
BAY LEAVES	TEJ PATTA
TURMERIC	HALDI
CORIANDER POWDER	DHANIYA POWDER
RIDGE GOURD	TORI
COURGETTE	ZUCCHINI
ASAFOETIDA	HEENG
FENUGREEK	METHI SEEDS
NUTMEG	JAIPHALL
GINGER	ADRAK
BASIL LEAVES	TULSI
MUSHROOM	KHUMB

Printed in the United States
By Bookmasters